Defeating the Struggle

Journal Entries of a Conqueror

By
Christopher B. Robinson

Copyright © 2019 Christopher B. Robinson

To contact the author: BreadTuckLegacy@gmail.com

Dedication

This book is dedicated to everybody who purchased this book. I want you to never give up and fight for your dreams. Never internalize other people's personal views of who you are.

Table of Contents

Introduction

Hello everybody! Welcome to *Defeating The Struggle*. If you are reading this, you are either super incredible, or you are taking steps to get there. This written empowerment content chronicles the steps that I have taken towards wanting to win big in life. I am not one of those guys that holds on to valuable information. If I experience something or learn something new, I am going to share it. I look at myself as a playmaker. I am a true point guard when it comes to life. I have absolutely no problem passing you the ball so that you can score…I just want the assist.

Do you mind if I share a little bit of my background? I will assume that you said yes. I haven't always thought like a winner. My mother pushed me to be great when I was younger. I just wasn't ready at the time that she was pushing me. I just wanted to be average. I just wanted to make it. As a high school student, I was horrible. By the time I reached my junior year, I had done so much damage that only a miracle could save me. My grade point average was somewhere along the lines of a 1.9. There was no way that I could graduate with my class. Even though I felt I had no options to make this right, I knew that I had to figure it out. There was no way I was going to miss the opportunity to walk that stage. I went to elementary school with those people who were guaranteed to graduate. They weren't going to move on without me. I had to make something happen. I found out something special about myself in this moment. I realized that I had determination. Even in wanting to be average, I realized that I was clutch.

Operation "Graduate On Time" was in full effect! I found ways to get this done. My counselor told me that I could graduate if I took freshman and senior classes my senior year. By that time, I was a junior. She was telling me what I had to do for the following year so in addition to that, I had to attend summer classes, my junior year. Walking across the stage with the people that I had grown up with was important to me. It took a miracle. With God and my willingness to work, it happened! I walked across that stage! June 1st of 2002 was an important day for me. On that date, I realized that I could have whatever I wanted! On that day, I also believed in miracles!

Let's switch gears for a second. I used to be the guy that wanted a government job. I wanted to work that job for 30 years and retire. This was my mindset coming out of high school. Years later, after high school, reality hit me! This isn't the 70's. This isn't your grandfather's world anymore. You can't depend on other people and jobs to take care of you. You have to have strong faith in God, number one!! After that, your mind has to be right. You have to be mentally on point, so that your body will follow. From there, you can take steps in a direction that will allow you to see things clearly and make calculated moves.

In this book, I am going to share with you the steps that allowed me to change my mindset. Once I got my mentality in position, I began to evolve as a human being. Once I reached 18, I was OF AGE. I could join the military, go to clubs, sign for credit cards, etc. In my late 20s, I changed my thoughts. I became a responsible, forward-thinking ADULT.

1

What is Discipline?

According to the Webster's Standard Dictionary, the word "discipline" means; a branch of knowledge or learning; formal training; self-control; acceptance of authority. For the context of this chapter, self-control will work. It is not easy to be disciplined. Look around you! Everything that you want is at your disposal. Fast food is cheap and affordable. Credit cards are easy to get. When your paycheck hits your account, there is a mall within reach. On the flip side, look at your body. Are you happy with it? If you aren't, it will take discipline to get it where you want it to be. If you want a summertime body, you have to watch what you eat. That means that the fast food that is so easily accessible may not be an option for you. To obtain this summertime body, you now have to cook and meal prep. You may not like the taste of the food you will need to eat. The taste of steamed carrots may not compare to the taste of a juicy cheeseburger. You have to make hard decisions. You have to figure out what is more important to you. Do you want a cheeseburger, or do you want to have that summertime body that you always wanted?

Let me speak to you about the credit card example. Credit cards are so easy to get. As soon as you turn 18, you start receiving applications for them. Why do we receive these applications so young? We are fresh out of high school. Our decision-making skills are not where they need to be yet. This is exactly why they send these applications to us so young. We don't know what it means to be fully disciplined yet so we look at that credit card as free money. All I have to do is walk in the store and swipe my card, I don't even need cash. I can buy the shoes that I always wanted. I can buy the concert tickets that I want. I can buy whatever it is I want, depending on how high my credit card limit is. You mean, I can spend $2,000, even if I don't have it? We don't consider the fact that we have to pay whatever we spend back. Not only that, you will have to pay a little extra on top of that. That is what you call interest. And if you're late, you have to pay late fees. This is why discipline is so important.

I just gave you a credit card and healthy eating example, but allow me put the spotlight back on myself and be transparent. In the introduction of this book, I talked about my struggles in high school. I had those struggles because I lacked discipline. I knew that we were supposed to go to high school for four years. I figured that I could purposely waste two of those years. I allowed high school to be a free-for-all. When it was time to go to class, I would skip school.

When it was time to study for a test, I would play games. I lacked structure. I only wanted to be disciplined when there was a goal in sight. It wasn't until I found out that graduating on time was out of the question that I was ready to do whatever it took. Now, we are getting somewhere.

Let's talk about the how. It's easy to tell people what they should do; it is another thing to tell them how. The most important thing is goal setting. What is your goal? Once you figure that out, put it in stone. Write it down. Write down the things it will take to make that goal attainable. Once you have written down what it takes to make that goal attainable, anything that gets in the way of that is a distraction. And when you understand that, you must be ready to sacrifice! Some of the things you love to do may not line up with your goals. Here is an example. Let's say that I have an issue with staying up late. My goal is to be in bed by 8pm Monday through Friday. I have to do whatever it takes, to be in bed by 8pm. After work, I need to come home, spend time with my family, cook, workout, etc. Only the important things should matter. I may have to sacrifice happy hour during the week, to make sure that the important things get done. If my favorite show comes on after 8, I will have to record it and watch it the next day at an earlier time. That is what you call discipline.

We must be disciplined. There are things in our lives that we are trying to achieve. To reach these goals, discipline must take place. Have you ever been to college? College is a beautiful experience. Your goal should be to get an education. While getting that education, you will notice that there will be parties, pretty girls, muscular guys, etc. If you are not disciplined, that will be a major distraction to your overall mission. Your mission is to get your degree and move on with your life. You will find yourself staying in college longer because you are not focused on what is most important. When you are disciplined, you focus and you execute. That takes self-control. I am not saying that you can't enjoy certain things, that's a part of life. You want to have fun, but there is this thing called moderation. Moderation is the avoidance of excesses or extremes.

If I have no discipline when using my credit card, I can put myself in a position to where I have bad credit. Bad credit is absolutely no good. You are looked at as being irresponsible when you have bad credit. The shoes, purse, concert tickets, etc. are not worth destroying your credit. Your credit needs to be intact for major purchases. Later on, you may want a house. Keep that in mind. That is way more important than the minor, trendy, materialistic purchases. Utilize discipline when making decisions. If you are a college student with a big test coming up, you don't need to party. You need to study. Have enough discipline to hit that party after you have aced your test. Some of us like alcohol. Drink it in moderation. Drink enough to where you can still function as a human being. Once you have reached that point of excessive drinking, bad things happen.

Apply discipline and moderation to your everyday life. Champions and people who are trying to be great are disciplined. They don't have time to watch TV all day. That is not a healthy diet for a champion. Greatness won't jump into you from a TV screen. What separates people from greatness is discipline. We all make choices. People who exude greatness got to where they are because they were committed to the idea of being great. Some of them would have loved to watch TV, shop, gossip, etc. all day. It sounds fun. Let me tell you the difference between great people and the average person. Great people know that in order to be great, sacrifices have to be made. You have to have self-control. Your mind has to be trained. You have to say NO when you want to say YES because you are aware of the outcome. That, my friend, is what you call discipline.

2

What Does Your Circle Look Like?

What you are about to read is important! Pay very close attention. The people that you choose to hang around will be seen as a reflection of you. Not only that, if you are still trying to figure things out about your life, you will take on the habits and personalities of the people around you. When we were in elementary, middle, and high school, we had no idea who we were as individuals. This is why we followed trends and wanted to be like other people. A lot of us even had cliques that we ran with. Let me again use myself as an example. I wanted to hang with the bad actors. I wanted to hang with the guys who sold drugs, smoked weed, and had all of the women. I was young. I wanted brand name athletic shoes and women. The bad actors were the types of guys that had both. In my mind, it made sense to hang with them.

As you get older and experience certain things, you have a better understanding of yourself. You also have a better understanding of the people that you have aligned yourself with. You begin to realize that you want different things out of life. You have different goals and you are on different paths. I am nowhere near the same guy that I was when I was 18. I am not even the same guy that I was five years ago. Watch where I am about to go with this. I am a 34-year-old man. Some of the people that I looked up to, act like they are still 18. I have evolved. I don't need that type of friendship. That is no good for me. Sometimes, people outgrow each other. There's nothing bad about it; that is just a part of life. You have groups of people that think like each other and have no desire to grow. Those types of people are made for each other. If you are truly trying to be better and the people around you are not, you should welcome separation.

Within your circle, you should expect your people to give you truth and vice versa. If I am looking crazy out here and you are my friend, you need to tell me. Friends should be able to respectfully keep it real. Tell me if I am slipping. Help me make corrections. You and your circle should help each other improve. If the goal is to be better, this should be ok.

Another reason you should check your circle is because, unfortunately, not everybody around you wants to see you win. If you are doing well, and your friends have no desire to grow, your "friends" will plot on you. You are making them look bad. It is possible that personal information you shared about your life with your friends will become public. Your "friends" can't stop your progress, but they will try to dirty your name. This can be avoided if you pay attention to who is around you. Pay attention to their reactions when you accomplish something big. Take mental notes on the regular. Also, your friends should lift you up! The people that you call your friends should be going out of their way to support you. If you have created something incredible, they should be helping you share that experience with the world. If your "friends" are leaving you to fend for yourself, that should be a red flag! Those people should be removed from your space. If they don't care about your success, you should get them out of your way. That relationship is not healthy. What you are about to read should be highlighted! Your friends do not have the power to stop your progress, but they do hold the power to propel you forward! If they are not propelling you forward, what is the point?

Why would you want people around you who don't celebrate your accomplishments? There are millions of people on this earth that don't care about you, and your friends should not resemble them. If you are a friend of mine, and your actions resemble the actions of people who care nothing about me, you've gotta go. Your circle should be tight. Based off of your interactions with your circle, people looking in should think that you are family. The people within your circle should have your back. In return, you should protect them and have their backs. If protection, celebration, and truth-telling aren't taking place, it's time to make cuts.

3

Block Other People's Loser Energy

When you think like a winner, you must remember that everybody does not think like you. You must hold yourself to a higher standard. You are not the norm. Your mindset is rare. Winning is not the average thought process. Everybody in the world would love to have your mindset. Unfortunately, some people are willing to either just get by or simply lose on a regular basis.

For me, I see myself as such a winner that I expect all things connected to me to win also. I live in Houston TX. I am a die-hard Texans and Rockets fan. I expect them to win a championship every year. I expect them to win every game that they play. Is that realistic? Absolutely not. But when you are trying to be great, you can't have an average thought process. This is how I am wired. I have conditioned myself to think like this.

You have to protect yourself from other people's loser energy. I would recommend not even hanging around people who don't mind losing. Don't get me wrong; we should help people. Some people may have never been exposed to the information that you have been exposed to. Maybe it is necessary for you to be around just to help change their mindset and that is OK. Some people are here to inspire. At the same time, if you notice that people are not willing to change, get as far away as possible. Pay attention to what you are about to read! Some people have made up in their mind that they are going to be experts at losing. When you notice that, your job is done. You must protect yourself. You are not there to carry that person out of "Loserville". People make choices in life. Protect the decision that you have made. Losing can be contagious if you allow it to be.

You will notice that once you have committed to winning, people who have made a commitment to losing will try and view you from their loser perspective. Don't you dare allow that! They will tell you what you can't do. People who have made a commitment to losing will view winners through the limitations that they set on themselves. You can't take it personally. They are not speaking to you, they are verbally speaking about their own abilities. They are just deflecting to you, because losers make excuses. Losers blame others for their mistakes. Losers notice your flaws but have no idea of their own. You must remind yourself that you are not one of them. You defy the odds. You are a superhero! You are a winner!

4

You Can't Please Everybody

I learned one of the most valuable lessons that anyone will ever learn. It doesn't matter how hard you try, you will not be able to please everybody. In your lifetime, you are going to meet many different types of people. And guess what?! Some of them won't like you. I had to realize that we all come from different parts of life. It is that simple. You will be in places mentally that others will never see. With that alone, people are not going to understand you. It's not a bad thing! Sometimes the cookie crumbles that way. You have to respect it and keep it moving.

Let me give you an example. I used to watch all types of reality shows that are no good for me. They didn't challenge me to grow. They didn't inspire me to progress towards greatness. Do those shows serve their purpose?

Yes, they do! They are meant for entertainment. Here is the thing, it wasn't the type of entertainment that I needed. I used to watch those shows and do funny recaps about them on social media, and I used to get all kinds of love. After I grew mentally and decided that I needed to leave those shows alone, I stopped watching them. From there, the recaps stopped. Some of the same people that were friends with me on social media began to unfriend me. At first, I used to take it personally. Then I began to see that it was all a part of my growth as a person.

As you grow and evolve, people are going to get rid of you. They are going to distance themselves from you. Some of your friendships will not make sense anymore because you won't be able to please them. That isn't always a bad thing. You may be heading towards different paths. Allow me to use the idea of leadership for an example, any type of leadership role that you can think of. Do you think that all leaders are liked by the people that they lead? Let me answer that for you…absolutely not! They have to make unpopular decisions. People who own businesses sometimes have to make budget cuts. That may result in pay cuts or loss of jobs. Not everybody is going to come out happy.

Look at your favorite singers, athletes, etc. Michael Vick is still hated to this day for fighting dogs. Let's not forget that the man did two years in prison for his crime. He paid his debt to society, but people still don't like him. I think the man should be forgiven. He should be able to live in peace. On the other hand, the people who don't really care for him have every right to feel how they do.

That just proves my point. Not everybody is going to like you. In other cases, a person disliking you may not even have anything to do with something you have done. People may not like your appearance or your personality. Either way, it's all good. Here is how you deal with that. You must develop thick skin. You must remain who you are. Most importantly, you must stay focused on your mission.

5

You Can't Base Your Life Decisions Off of the Lives of Others

In life, we have free will to make our own choices. Often times, we are inspired by others. Then there are times when we look at others as an example. People can serve as an example to us, whether it be good or bad. Example, let's say that I had the desire to rob a bank. I figure out a plan on how I will do it. Then I turn on the news and see that somebody robbed a bank, got caught, and is about to serve prison time. If I am wise, I will learn from that and use that example to help make the best decision possible. If I am smart, I probably won't rob that bank. The risk is way too dangerous. You can't put a value on your freedom. This example is an extreme example that deals with morals and values.

Here is something that people do that I will never understand. People will not act on a particular idea because somebody who acted on something similar may not have been successful at it. For example, I know a person that wanted to start a business. Unfortunately, he decided not to start a business because he saw somebody else fail at it. In this situation, there are a few things that we must realize. #1 We do not know what is going on in the next person's life. That person may be dealing with something that you are not dealing with and that particular situation may have played a part in them not being successful. #2 You might have a little more knowledge or insight than the person that you are basing your moves after. #3 You and the person you are basing your moves after are two different people. That is the most important thing. You two are not going to do things the same way. For example, if you give two people the same instructions to bake a cake, there is a strong possibility that those cakes may come out tasting differently. One person might add a little more sugar. The other person may want extra flour. We are all individuals. If we are truly being ourselves, our situations and experiences won't be exactly the same.

I think that it is ok to look at people as examples. You can even look at people and learn from their mistakes. We must not get in the habit of looking at others like their experiences are the be all and end all though. Sometimes, we give other people way too much credit. In fact, we give them way more credit than we give ourselves. Go for yours!

I don't care whose marriage failed! I don't care whose business failed! You may know a person who flunked out of college. Who cares? We can't let other people's failures predict our next move. Remember, you are a winner! You were not put on this Earth to live in fear. You were put on this Earth to show others how it was meant to be done! Trust your gut! If you have a vision or idea, go for it!

6

Stay Close To What Inspires You

When I originally had the thought to write this book, I was overjoyed about it. For the first time, I actually had a solo idea that I could execute and be proud of. With the original concept that I came up with, I just knew I was going to do something amazing. Then I allowed the most dangerous thing to happen to my fresh idea. I allowed time to pass. In letting this time pass, I did everything else except focus on my book. In my world, I have one gift. This one gift of mine is the only thing that will take me to the next level in my life. This gift is the main reason that I exist on this Earth. I have the gift of painting pictures/visuals with my words. In that regard, I am an artist. I don't have the ability to hit a game-winning 3-pointer with 3 seconds left on the clock. I don't have the ability to throw a 65-yard Touchdown. My gift is in writing.

With that said, I still allowed time to pass. My inspiration to write this book was deteriorating. The other FOOLISHNESS in my life was taking over. It got to a point where writing a book was not even on my radar. Then one day, I thought about it. I want to be great. I am inspired by GREATNESS. I made a conscious decision to let go of some of the foolishness that I was participating in, so that I could make room for GREATNESS. I had to stop watching foolishness on the television, and dedicate that time to reading about great people. If I did watch TV, I needed to watch the Shark Tank. I needed to watch documentaries on Muhammad Ali. I needed to listen to podcasts that would challenge me to be better. These are examples of things that inspire me.

If you have distractions in your life, you have to get rid of them. Distractions are there to impede progress. We all have goals. Some of us have short-term goals. Some of us have long-term goals. Some of us have short and long-term goals. Do you know how focused you have to be to reach your goals? When you are really focused, distractions are going to come from everywhere. Some distractions, you may not have any control over. For example, you may be working on a project in your home, while your neighbor is throwing a party and blasting loud music. Then there will be other distractions that you will have 100% control over. Like you are working on your project, but you stop working to attend the party.

If you are studying to be a pharmacist, you may need to sacrifice your TV for a while. You need to be around inspiration. After you study, you may need to drive by the Walgreen's pharmacy. That will feed your hunger to get it done. If you are trying to write books, you may want to join a writers' club and hang out at bookstores. Do you want to create films? You need to make your way to film festivals. Figure out what inspires you and attach yourself to activities that relate to your inspiration. You need to feel that energy! That energy is going to feed your passion. When your energy feeds your passion, you can focus more on the mission.

When you stay close to what inspires you, you will find a way to feed your inspiration! Don't allow your inspiration to go hungry!

7

Lead By Example

Have you ever heard or taken advice from somebody that has never experienced what they are telling you to do? That sounds ridiculous. You have to be credible when you are giving advice or trying to lead a person. You can't just tell a person to do something, and you have nothing backing you as to why they should listen to you. Would you trust a mechanic who always has a broken down car? I don't know about you, but I would want to know why his car is broken down before we even worry about my car. If you are a mechanic with a beat up car, your credibility is a little shaky. Would you let a barber cut your hair if his hair is all over the place? I wouldn't dare. I would have a million questions. You are a barber, right? Your hair should always be on point. Do you own a pair of clippers? Do you know other barbers? Would you take relationship advice from a person who is in and out of relationships? I wouldn't. Don't get me wrong; I would still learn from them. I would watch that person and learn what NOT to do.

We have to be mindful when somebody is telling us something. Check their credibility and watch their fruits. There is an old saying that actions speak louder than words. That is so true. People will often give you advice that they will never follow. People will tell you to leave your mate, but they don't have the heart to leave theirs. People will tell you to quit your job and start a business, but the person telling you this is still employed. It is easy for a person to give hero advice, but I have a question. Has that person ever been a hero?

It is time for people to start leading by example. When you are doing what you are asking others to do, you have credibility. I am no Lakers' fan, but look at a guy like Kobe Bryant. Every time he stepped out onto the court, he gave 200%. He had every right to get upset with his teammates if they weren't giving their all. That is leadership by example. If I am a manager at a restaurant, I shouldn't ask my staff to do something that I wouldn't do. I shouldn't ask them to do something that I have never done. That is weak and pathetic. When you set the standard and act as an example, the people around you become INSPIRED.

On my social media platforms, I push my friends and followers to go after their dreams. I push them to walk out their visions. I am qualified to do that, because I am presenting myself as a living example. I am showing them that I am going after my dreams and visions also. When I fall, I let them know about it. When I have success, I let them know about it. I document it and put it out there. I am making sure that I am presenting myself as a living example.

I was having a conversation with my good friend. We were talking about leadership. He told me that leadership is inspirational. That is so true. When you are leading, you will have to give verbal directions. That is a given. But how do your actions look? If people are not inspired by you being in front, you need to reevaluate how you do things. You may just be a dictator or somebody who talks just for the sake of talking. I saw a meme on social media that was very powerful. The meme was divided in half, horizontally. The top half of the meme had a general sitting in the back, while a bunch of other soldiers ran out in front with guns, ready to fight. The bottom half of the picture had the general out in front leading while his troops followed. Within the bottom half of the meme, the caption said, "true leadership". When you lead by example, you are visible. Being a visible leader will get you respect.

8

Make Great Use of Your Time

I had the idea to write a self-help book back in 2010. I had a general idea of what I wanted to write about. I had the chapters lined up as soon as the idea to write a book came to me. At the time this chapter was written, it was October of 2015. I sat on this idea for 5 years. I had the content to write about, I just moved at a ridiculously slow pace. I am still clueless as to why I was dragging my feet when I was supposed to be writing this. Of course, chapters that I wanted to write about have changed over the course of those years. I have had different experiences throughout these five years. I can even go so far as to say that have I released this book sooner than when I did, it would not have been as detailed. My perspective is way different from when I originally started writing this chapter. Even in saying all of that, I still should have been documenting information about my experiences. Documenting my perspective is what I wasn't doing. But I will tell you what I was doing within that time. I was watching reality TV. I was social networking. I was documenting recaps of reality TV while social networking. I was working a second job that I should have moved on from. My focus was all over the place. My focus was on everything else, except for where it was supposed to be. In the grand scheme of things, my time management was off. I was focused on everything else, except for what my purpose was. I wasted years of my time doing things that I have no interest in doing now.

When you look at life, sometimes you can see exactly why people are nowhere near where they are supposed to be. They spend their time being unfocused. Why are some college students in school way too long? They may spend the majority of their time partying and bull crapping! I am an expert on that. It took me six years to get my Associate's Degree. When most of your time is used to party, when do you study? There is an old saying that will make this make sense. If you want to master something, you have to put 10,000 hours into it. Why do we find ourselves having a passion for something but we put our passion on hold? I will tell you the reason. We are not inspired. We would rather spend our time focusing on nonsense. It is our job to stay close to things that inspire us. If you want to be a movie writer, you need to study other great movie writers. You need to figure out what those before you have done to achieve great success. Do you want to be great? It is inspiring to see a person that you admire winning in your field.

To be great, we must spend our time wisely. We have to remove ourselves from what others are doing. Their focus and your focus may be totally different. The people you are hanging around may not have a problem with being average. When you don't have a problem with being average, forget about greatness. You have time to focus on things that don't matter. To be great, you have to utilize your time wisely. You have to utilize the time you would normally set aside for foolishness to focus on being better. Sean "Puff Daddy" Combs is worth several hundreds of millions of dollars. That is not what makes him great. His achievements that led to the fortune is what is most impressive. I watched him in an interview one day. The most important piece of information that I took away from that interview was him saying, "I have 24 hours in a day like everybody else." That let me know that time is one of the most valuable items we have on this Earth. Use your time wisely.

9

Create Options

From 2008 to 2012, I worked a particular job where I felt trapped. I had options, but my options were few. I remember riding in the back of a work-van with no seats. Work equipment was falling on top of me. I felt worthless. I began to talk to myself. I asked myself a couple of questions. Who lives like this? Who works like this? What mistakes did I make along the way to put myself in the back of a work-van with equipment falling on me? Why do the guys in the front have seats and I don't? At that moment, my life did not make sense to me. I knew that I had to do something about it.

That same week, I went to an open house for the University of Houston Downtown. The following week, I was enrolled in school. I still worked that job, but my future looked brighter. They finally gave us a work-truck with four seats. That wasn't enough for me. I still had to have a plan to get out.

I worked that ridiculous job from 7 a.m. - 3 p.m. Monday through Friday. From there, I would take college classes at night. I gave myself two years to get my degree to create options for myself. In exactly two years, I had earned my degree. I then became "overqualified" for the job that I was working. I continued to work there, as I looked for other employment. Later on, while still working there, I found a second job to create more income.

While working both jobs, the supervisors at my primary job began to treat me bad. They were doing this because I had more education than them. I could feel the jealousy. The other employees were stuck there. They were treated horribly, but they felt like they had no other choice but to take it. They didn't equip themselves with tools to create options. This particular, meaningless job was all they had known. One night in 2011, I was collecting my thoughts at 11 p.m. I made up in my mind that this job was not coming with me into 2012. That same night, I wrote up my two-week notice and turned it in the following day. My supervisor was looking at me with surprise. He didn't expect people to quit this job. He knew that the people there were mentally trapped. Not me, I was out and didn't look back. I felt like my options had increased. I FELT UNSTOPPABLE!!!!!

The best way for you to create options is through education. When you read, you take in information that belongs to you. If others want to know what you know, they will seek you. You then have power. Nobody can take that from you. Learn a new skill. When you are able to do things that others can't do, others will have to pay you for your services. Treat people kindly and maintain healthy relationships with people. You may not know what the person that you are talking to is working on. You maintain a healthy relationship with that person, and he or she may be able to help elevate you later on in life. That person can assist in getting you into a better situation.

It is important to create options for yourself because you gain leverage when you do so. Options give you power. In whatever you do, don't allow yourself to be limited. When you are limited, you will find yourself trapped. When I worked the job that I was just speaking about, I used to talk with my co-workers. I used to ask them about the dreams and visions that they may have. The responses from them were sad to hear. They had been stuck in that job so long that they lost themselves. They weren't able to express other ideas. All they wanted to do was get promoted, but they lacked the education to do so. Their options were few. To avoid being POWERLESS and trapped, do yourself a favor and create options for yourself.

10

Find Your 'Chillion'

I was talking to a good friend of mine over the phone. His name is Ian Giddens. That brotha is a deep-thinking brotha like myself. I like to connect with guys who have similar conversation and similar types of energy. In our conversation, he said something I thought was amazing. We were talking about farming, growing our own food, and being independent. We also began to talk about how much money we will need to stop working for somebody else. We were trying to figure out our individual number that would allow us to comfortably take care of our families. This is where Ian said something that I found to be amazing. He asked me, "What is your 'chillion'?" He explained to me that a 'chillion' is the amount of money you need to take care of yourself and your family for the rest of your lives. You can chill forever.

If you were to sit down and think about that number, it

would all make sense. That number must also be realistic. For example, my number is 5 million dollars. This is my personal number. So let me break that number down for you. From this 5 million, I expect taxes to take half of that. I have never been in this tax bracket, but I hear what happens with people who are making this type of money. I will just go with half of my 5 million being taken from me. This leaves me with 2 1/2 million dollars. I believe in God, so I will use $500,000 to pay my tithes and help others. About $180,000 will pay my house off. $80,000 will take care of my family's student loans. I will set aside $50,000 to splurge. From this 5 million, this leaves me with 1,690,000 dollars. I believe that 5% interest of this number should be enough for me and my family to live on. With a home fully paid off and absolutely no debt, a little over $80,000 a year should be more than enough. I will also make other investments from this $50,000 that will be used to splurge.

Think about it. There are people who make less than $80,000 yearly, and they have mass amounts of debt. These people have car notes, rent/mortgage, loans, kids, amongst other things. Imagine if all you had to pay for were your kids and the property taxes on your home. It would be less stressful and way easier to help your family members who need you financially. When you find your chillion, you will be in a comfortable space.

Now that you know this, the next step is figuring out a way to get to your chillion. Here is a little more perspective for you. Would you rather work 30 years, then retire from a job that will only pay you so much money every month?

Let's keep in mind that today, retiring after 30 years isn't a guarantee anymore. Machines are replacing human beings. Apps and online stores are eliminating the average worker. Let's just say you are fortunate to make it to 30 years. By the time you are able to get those benefits from that job, you are 30 years older. Wouldn't you rather just find your chillion?

I am taking my own advice. I am a school teacher. I love my job, but as teachers we are not paid what we are worth. I don't plan on teaching for 30 years. I need more out of life, and I have more to offer. I love writing. I also have a love for speaking to and in front of people. These are my loves, so I had to figure out ways to monetize them. This book that you are reading is one way. I also have created my own paid speaking engagements. Then there is podcasting. The Bread Tuck Legacy Podcast is a weekly show that I produce. I speak on current events and find the message within the topic. These are things that I do for free, but I am trying to create a revenue stream from them. If one of my hobbies becomes a hit and I generate 5 million dollars, I'm onto something. You have to give yourself a shot. Why not? What do you have to lose other than the next 30 years working for someone else?

Reaching that number may not take you 30 years. Imagine reaching this number in less than 5 years. Depending on how old you are, you can still be young enough to enjoy your fruits! A lot of times, I see old men driving these nice sports cars. I often assume that they just retired and that is their retirement gift to themselves. I could be wrong. Why not work extremely hard for yourself? Why not do whatever it is that you love to do? Why not find a way to monetize your passion? I know for a fact that life is more fulfilling that way. The bottom line is, if we can figure out a way to find that chillion, life becomes that much more relaxing. Suddenly, you don't have to tolerate DISRESPECT from a job anymore. Suddenly, you begin to feel free with less pressure. Finding that chillion doesn't sound like a bad idea, huh?

11

Be Your Own Hero

I am a superhero fanatic. When I was a child, I wanted to be a superhero. I looked up to superheroes. Every chance that I got, I would watch them on television. I enjoyed watching Spiderman, Superman, Batman, etc. on TV. As I grew older and began to understand life, I began to realize something. None of these characters looked like me. I am an African-American male, and the majority of the heroes on television were white. A lot of people will say that color does not matter, but yes, it does! Representation is important. Younger children of different cultures should have superheroes that they can relate to culturally. I would sit at home and wonder where the black superheroes were.

From that point, I began to read comic books. I found out that we had black superheroes. T'Challa, King of Wakanda! He took over the mantle of Black Panther when his father died. We had Luke Cage, a bulletproof black man who watches over Harlem. Jefferson Pierce, a school principal by day, Black Lightning at night. John Stewart, the Black-American Green Lightning. John Henry Irons, an X Military weapons maker and Black-American Superman! I can go on for days. The only difference is, our superheroes were not put on television at the time.

You all might think that I am crazy for saying this, but in my mind, I created my own superhero. I became that superhero. Of course, I could not go out fighting crime, jumping in front of cars, and things of that nature. In my mind, I followed the principles of being a superhero. Unless you are talking about anti-heroes who are known to go against the grain, pretty much all superheroes live by the same principles. They treat people fairly, they are kind to people, and they give their all in what they do. They live by more principles, but for the sake of this text, I had to give fitting examples.

In the real world, there is no such thing as superheroes, but we have real-life heroes that we look up to. Some of us look up to our parents. Some of us look up to firemen, policemen, military, teachers, etc. There is absolutely nothing wrong with that. One day, it hit me, why can't I become my own hero? I don't mean this in a vain way. What I am saying is, I can become the person that I would look up to. The principles that I respect in other people, I can add them to my life and live by those principles.

While you're living these principle, you will have trials and tribulations that try to get in the way. For example, I aim to be a person who lets close to nothing get me upset. That is not an easy task, but it is one of my ultimate goals.

The main reason why this task is difficult for me is that I cannot stand people who have bad attitudes for no reason. That really gets under my skin. I am trying to get to a point where, even though it may upset me, I will not get out of character.

Be your own hero; strive to be the person that has the qualities that you would like to obtain. I am not saying imitate another person, I am saying that you should create the person in your mind that you want to be and work at being him or her. If you smoke and you want to be a person who does not smoke at all, you can do that. Take strides at quitting. You may be a person who is physically out of shape, but you want to be a person who is in tip-top shape. I believe that you can be that person. It will not be an easy task. However, if you get your mind and your body ready to do some serious work, you can get it done. Don't let anybody tell you anything different.

If I may use The Batman as an example for a minute, I will share information that can help put this thing into perspective. Unlike Superman, Spiderman, The Hulk and other superheroes, Batman does not have powers that he was born with. He does not have powers that were given to him through some type of experiment gone wrong. Batman had to go through intense training and put time into gaining his skills. I know that Batman is a fictional character, but take that and apply that to your everyday life. Be your own hero!

12

There is POWER in Loss

I have lost two extremely important people in my lifetime! I lost my grandmother and my mother. My grandmother's name is Girtha Marie Robinson. I have her first name tattooed down my right leg. I did that because I want her to help guide my path. She was a major influence on me. My mother's name is Vira Jean Copeland. I have her name tattooed on my left wrist. I want her spirit to guide my hands. I want to bring life into everything that I touch. These women are my heroes. Even though these two amazing women have left this Earth, their spirits still live through me. This is why I use the words is and are, when talking about them. My grandmother died in January of 2004, and my mother died in September of 2007. I lost my heroes 3 years apart from each other.

Although my grandmother has passed, I still feel Girtha Marie Robinson has my back. My grandmother and I will continue to have a deep bond. When I was a little boy, I lived in Mississippi with her. My mother had just gotten married to my "stepdad". His name is Harold. Harold and my mother lived overseas during my early childhood, because my "stepdad" served in the military. I use quotation marks because I recognize him as my father. Harold J. Copeland is the man who played basketball with me, taught me how to drive, among other things. He took on that role when my biological father did not. With that said, Harold will forever be my father! Now that we've cleared that up, let's get back to The Great Girtha Marie!

We used to watch TV together and everything! We enjoyed each other's company. On Saturday nights, we would watch TV together. Around the mid to late 90's, we would watch the CBS Saturday night lineup. Touched by an Angel, Early Edition, and Walker Texas Ranger. We looked forward to Saturday nights. We also watched the Houston Rockets together. At this time, the Rockets were broadcasted on UPN 20 which existed before what is now the CW Network. I was always by my grandmother's side. She drove this old Cadillac and kept a gun on her. She was fearless. Girtha Marie was "Bout it, Bout it." If you don't know what "Bout it, Bout it" is, google it.

Around 2000, I began to notice a decline in her health. I didn't know exactly what was going on. All I knew at that time was I had her back. During that time period, my mother, younger brother and myself lived with my grandmother. She was leasing a two-story townhome. My dad was living in New York at this time. He was still in the military, and he was also separated from my mother. I was attending Westbury High School. I had to wake up early, every morning, because I would have to ride the bus to school. Not only did I wake up to catch the bus, but I woke up to help my grandmother get dressed. My grandmother didn't want the rest of my family to know what was going on. My aunts, mom, uncles, and other family members had an idea, but I knew everything. My grandmother trusted me. Waking up to help her was humbling. I had to help her use the restroom, in addition to helping her get dressed. As a teen, I sacrificed a lot. I was perfectly fine with that. I knew that she would have done the same for me.

Eventually, my family found out the details of what was happening with my grandmother. By that time, my dad had retired from the military and moved to Houston to work things out with my mom. My dad, mom, brother and myself moved into our own apartment around 2001. At that time, I had to transfer high schools and be away from my grandmother. I hated it, but she moved into a better situation with my Aunt Eunice. My Aunt Eunice had a bigger living space and more resources to help my grandmother. On Saturdays, I would go visit and spend the night at my Aunt Eunice's house. I would still help my grandmother use the restroom when necessary. When it came time for my grandmother to go to sleep, my Aunt Eunice would get her ready for bed.

By January of 2004, I had a driver's license and I had been working for about 3 years. I was able to drive to my Aunt's house. I was a waiter at a restaurant. During one of my off days, I remember getting a call from my Aunt Eunice. She told me that my grandmother was in the hospital and it was serious. I rushed to the hospital, to see my grandmother hooked up to a machine. She was on life support. Five minutes into me being there, my grandmother had passed away. My grandmother had a disease known as Lou Gehrig's disease. This disease is also known as ALS. ALS is a nervous system disease that weakens muscles and impacts physical functioning. I remember driving home and taking a nap. I didn't cry or anything. I missed my grandmother, but in a way, it was a relief. I didn't have to see her like that anymore. Most importantly, she didn't have to suffer any longer.

My mother, Vira Jean, was one of a kind. She was different from my grandmother, in regard to how she treated me. She was tough on me. At times, I think she was overly tough. I truly believe that she was getting me ready for this cold world. I was closer to my grandmother than I was my mother. That lady was mean. She was extremely strict with me. I couldn't listen to rap music in the house. I couldn't hang with my friends outside of school. I couldn't do anything. One thing about me is, I always found a way to do what I wanted. I would lie and sneak to get what I wanted. I remember wanting to go to a party. I told my mom that I was going to the barbershop. I left the house around 5 pm on a Saturday night. I didn't get back until 12 AM. My mom was heated! She was now in a wheelchair. She couldn't physically do much to me, but her verbal ability to let me have it was just as bad. My dad knew I was full of crap. He wasn't as upset as my mom, but he was mad. His reason for being mad was different. He was mad because he had to deal with my mom being mad.

Even though my mother was unreasonably mean, she pushed me to be great. At the time of her pushing me to be great, I wasn't mentally ready or mature enough to achieve greatness. As a child, my mother drilled academics into my brother and I. I wasn't hearing any of that! I wanted clothes, cool shoes, and female attention. Also, I thought it was cool to not know as much. Thank God for growth! Writing that sentence just feels stupid. I was naturally smart. If I would have applied myself, I would have been unstoppable! Instead, I chose to be average! I remember being tested in high school to be in honors classes. I performed high on the test, and I was placed in the honors classes. This happened, because my mother fought for me. Before she fought for me to be in honors, this same school wanted to test me for special education.

As I reflect on this, I wish my mother never fought for me. All I did was let her down. I went to those honors classes and became lazy! I didn't want to do the extra work. The school had a meeting, to speak about my performance. I remember my mother breaking down and crying in front of the teachers and administrators. My mother did her part. I didn't do what I was supposed to do. I felt like such a loser. I felt like scum! After this meeting, I gave minimal effort to try and pass that semester. The damage was already done. It wasn't much I could do. I was held back.

That was my 10th-grade year. A lot was going on during this time. My grades sucked, and my conduct was trash! Why did I even bother going to school? All I did was make other people's job difficult. The school was gearing up to send me to an alternative school, but my mother decided to send me to another school. I transferred to Sharpstown high school. My mother figured a new start would help me. Boy, was she right! New scenery, along with my amazing grandmother paying for summer school resulted in me graduating on time! I walked across the stage with the people that I had grown up with! It felt great to overcome adversity and still make it across the stage. I even went on to college. I wanted to go to Prairie View University like a lot of my friends. Vira Jean shut that down with the quickness! I had to claw and scratch to get out of high school! There was no way I was going to focus while at a university miles away from my home. Community college it was! I was Houston Community College bound!

I caught the bus to Houston Community College to get my paperwork done. My mother actually trusted me to figure it out! Well, not really. She had to work, so I had to attempt to be an adult for once. I remember waiting all day in the financial aid office. They told me that they were out of money. I didn't even ask questions. I was prepared to accept no for an answer. I called my mom and told her what was going on. I then told her that I would just work at the restaurant for a semester. She told me to stay there. I don't know how she did it, but my mother made it across town in 10 minutes! She knew that if I didn't keep the ball rolling with school, I would have been doomed! She spoke to the financial aid people and an hour later, I was enrolled in school for the coming semester.

A year later, while I was in school, I noticed that my mother's health had gotten bad. Vira Jean was a healthy, energetic woman, who now needed a walker to get around.

I didn't understand it. Her health had only gotten worse from there. She went from a walker to a wheelchair. From the wheelchair, she later became confined to a bed, while being hooked to breathing tubes. I was confused, but I still had hope. By this time, I was working two jobs. I was a teacher assistant in the morning, and a waiter in the evening. This was around mid-2007. I had hope because my mother was in great spirits! She knew that she was coming out of this! She encouraged everybody who came to visit her! She couldn't even speak. She had a dot on her head that communicated with this machine. She would use the dot to spell out what she had to say. One of the most memorable moments was when I visited her on my birthday in 2007. As soon as I walked into the room, she sang Happy Birthday to me. No sound came from her mouth, but I could read her lips. That was one of the greatest gifts that my mother had ever given me.

Around late October, early September of 2007, my mother was being prepared to leave the hospital. She was going to have medical assistance while living with my Aunt Vera. My Aunt Vera and my mother were twins. They were super close. My mom was still confined to a bed and hooked to a breathing machine, but she was showing some improvement. We were excited. We were finally beginning to see the light. Then, on September 5th of 2007, I received the worst phone call that I had ever received! My Aunt Vera called me to tell me that my mother had passed away. I was at my morning job. I didn't know what to do. I was confused. I didn't expect her to die. My mother had me feeling that she was going to beat this sickness that had come over her. My mother passed from a disease called Guillain-Barre Syndrome. Guillain-Barre is an autoimmune condition in which the person's nerves are attacked by the body's own immune defense system.

When my mother passed away, I was in the middle of taking a break from school. I didn't really have time to work. I was working a full-time and part-time job. I had rent, car note, and other bills to pay. At that time, I also had a girlfriend, who is now my wife. I was only one class away from my Associate's Degree. I was around 23 years old. I knew that she would have wanted me to finish school. I also think that she knew I would finish eventually. I had gotten too close to not finish. My mother's passing expedited this school process. I wasn't sure if I was ready to commit to getting my four-year degree, but I knew it was time to grab this Associate's Degree by the horns! Within a year of my mother dying, I obtained my Associate's Degree. Two years after that, I obtained my Bachelor's Degree.

After the combined passing of my grandmother and mother, I took on a fearless attitude! At this period in life, I had lost the two most valuable people ever. I didn't lose a car, money, or home...those things can be replaced. I lost my mother and my grandmother. The two women who knew me best were now gone. That put things into perspective for me. Material possessions no longer matter to me! In life, I now play with house money. Betting it all, and losing material things don't matter. What can be worse than losing your mother?

There is Power in Loss! Think about this. When you lose a job for the first time, there is no reason to fear that feeling anymore. You already felt that. You know how to deal with that if it happens again. If you have never been punched before, you are going to be scared to fight! Once you take a punch, you know how it feels! Of course, you want to avoid it. But if it happens, so what! Did you die? If you lived through loss, you are now stronger! You are now able to help others get through a similar situation! You are an expert on what to look out for.

When you deal with a major loss, take that hurt and turn it into something great! You automatically have the edge on others! They have never felt the pain that you have felt! Not only did you go through it, but you lived to tell your story. There is tremendous value in this! Use that fuel to empower yourself, build a legacy for yourself and your family! Always remember that there is Power in Loss!

13

Identify and Understand Your Reason Why

When I was younger, I had immature and selfish reasons for wanting to be financially successful. I wanted to have a lot of money so that I could be seen as "the man". I wanted an exotic car. I wanted designer brands. I knew that if I was financially successful, I could afford these things. I wanted to have these material things only for others to notice me. This was my mindset while I was in my late teens to early twenty's.

Around age 25, I began to not to care as much for material items. Around this time, I was introduced to a more mature way of thinking. I began to look at the big picture. There was no more time to focus on only what was in front of me. I had gotten married and knew that my family would expand one day. With a newly changed mindset, my goals changed. I was no longer wanting exotic cars, flashy clothes and other foolishness. I wanted property, investments, money market accounts, and Roth IRAs. I wanted something that I could leave to my future kids.

On October 2nd of 2018, my greatest creation made her debut. Nyla Brielle Robinson was born at 2:25 pm. She was 6 pounds and 7 ounces. My reasoning for wanting to be successful is completely different nowadays. Don't get me wrong. My thinking matured a long time ago, but Nyla Brielle has me more focused than I have ever been. With my daughter, I can't imagine working two jobs. Nyla needs my attention. She needs my protection. She needs her father in this ruthless world. When she calls, I will be on my way no matter what.

As a father, my "Reason Why" is clearer than it has ever been. Why do I want to go so hard to achieve success? Nyla Brielle Robinson is the answer. I can't imagine her going without. I refuse to allow that. She will have everything that all of the other kids have. As a matter of fact, she will have more. I don't want her to deal with struggle. This is why I must defeat it! Do you like what I did there?

She is my reason why. You must determine your reason. When you find yourself wanting something, ask yourself why you want it. Is it worth the work? Your reason must be clear to you. I don't believe that one person can motivate another person. One person can inspire another person. One person can do something that provokes the other person to think. Motivation comes from within. If you take the time to discover your reason why, you will figure it out.

Imagine you are a high school athlete, who wants to play division one sports. You will have to sacrifice and work ridiculously hard. What would be your reason for working ridiculously hard? You would work ridiculously hard because you want to be a division one college athlete. Wanting to be a division one college athlete would be your why. I get it. Not all of us can relate to being division one college athletes. Let me give you a more relatable example. Imagine you are a hard working employee. You are never late, you are overworked, underpaid, and underappreciated. After years of working in this toxic environment, you decide that you want to work for yourself. You have this brilliant idea to start a window cleaning business. You make up in your mind that you will be relentless. Nothing in this world will keep you from making this happen. You decide that you would rather work for yourself. You decide that you want to make your own rules. Your reason why is simple. You do not want to go back to being overworked, underpaid, underappreciated, and overlooked. Now you are willing to do what it takes to avoid that.

Determine your reason for wanting to be great. Determine your reason for wanting to change your life for the better. That is important. When you are trying to accomplish whatever it is that you are trying to do, it is going to get tough. Your reason why will keep you focused. Your reason why will push you when you want to give up. When I hold my daughter, she has this peaceful look on her. She freely lays in my arms and looks up at the ceiling. She looks as if she is safe from all harm. I can't blame her at all! She is correct! She will be protected at all cost. It is my job to make sure she is successful. I wouldn't have it any other way! She is my "Reason Why"!

Closing

I want to thank everyone who purchased this book. Your reason to purchase this book may have only been to support me, or maybe you were someone who needed a breakthrough in your life, and you took a chance on this book. Either way, I want to say thank you for giving me a shot. Writing this book was not the easiest thing to do. There were plenty of moments where I had to stop writing this book for long periods of time. I began writing this book around 2011 and many of my original ideas have changed since then. I will say this, 2019 was the perfect time for me to release this book. Had I released this book sooner, it would have been incomplete.

I want every reader to read this book and become inspired. If you were already inspired before reading this, I want you to apply action along with being inspired. Many people wake up daily only to continue to be unhappy with their situation. The sad thing is, people are conditioned to just deal with being unhappy. With that said, leave here and apply action to your life. If your situation sucks, then take steps to figure out a solution. You are in control…never forget that.

29090141R00044

Made in the USA
Lexington, KY
25 January 2019